BEYOND THE GENDER BINARY

ALOK VAID-MENON

PENGUIN WORKSHOP

This book is dedicated to everyone who has ever been made to feel like they were too much or never enough—AVM

PENGUIN WORKSHOP
An Imprint of Penguin Random House LLC, New York

The publisher does not have any control over and does not assume any responsibility for author or third-party websites or their content.

Text copyright © 2020 by Alok Vaid-Menon. Illustrations copyright © 2020 by Penguin Random House LLC. All rights reserved. Published by Penguin Workshop, an imprint of Penguin Random House LLC, New York. PENGUIN and PENGUIN WORKSHOP are trademarks of Penguin Books Ltd, and the W colophon is a registered trademark of Penguin Random House LLC. Manufactured in China.

Visit us online at www.penguinrandomhouse.com.

Library of Congress Cataloging-in-Publication Data is available upon request.

ISBN 9780593094655   10 9 8 7 6 5 4 3 2 1

PROLOGUE

This is a book about the gender binary. Specifically, why we need to move beyond it. The gender binary is a cultural belief that there are only two distinct and opposite genders: man and woman. This belief is upheld by a system of power that exists to create conflict and division, not to celebrate creativity and diversity.

We deserve more options. This false choice of boy or girl, man or woman, male or female is not natural—it is political. The real crisis is not that gender non-conforming people exist, it's that we have been taught to believe in only two genders in the first place.

Gender diversity is an integral part of our existence. It always has been, and it always will be.

There is a shocking disconnect between the way the government and the media speak about gender non-conforming people and the reality of our lives. This gap between representation and reality continues to get worse. As we face heightened prejudice and harassment on the ground, more policies and public statements deriding us continue to be made. This disconnect is not a coincidence; it is a calculation. This is how it has always worked: The best way to eliminate a group is to demonize them, such that their disappearance is seen as an act of justice, not discrimination.

But this *is* about discrimination, and it's time that we address it. The reality that many gender non-conforming people cannot go outside without fear of being attacked is unacceptable. The issue is not that we are failing to be men or women. It's that the criteria used to evaluate us to begin with is the problem.

BEYOND THE GENDER BINARY

The days that I feel most beautiful are the days that I am most afraid.

They tell us to "be ourselves," but if you listen closely, there's more to that sentence: ". . . until you make them uncomfortable."

Be yourself until you make them uncomfortable.

There is always a limit. A breaking point. Once you cross the line, then you are "too much" and are put back in your place.

In this way, acceptance of self-expression becomes conditional. Express yourself using this template under these constraints with this time limit. Go! It's like being handed over a Scantron sheet and demanded to paint a self-portrait on it. It's possible, of course, but why even bother when a canvas is within our reach?

Is it really a choice when you don't get to select the options you are given to begin with?

The other day, I left the house wearing a teal dress, purple lipstick, and a full beard. I have always—and I mean always—loved color. If you flip through our old family photo albums, it'll feel like sifting through the pages of a fashion magazine. There I am at five years old, wearing a vibrant floral print T-shirt with fuchsia shorts, a pink lunch box, and a huge smile to top it all off.

What I like about colors is that when you mix them together, they become greater than the sum of their parts, something different altogether. No one goes around asking, "But are you really more *blue* or more *green*?" Teal is not blue-green, it is *teal*.

But I'm getting ahead of myself here. Back to the other day. I have to admit it was foolish of me to leave the house in that dress. New York winters are unforgivingly cold, but there I was, with no coat, trekking through the streets on my way to the grocery store.

As I walked down Sixth Avenue, two people started pointing and shouting, "That's a man in a dress! Hey, everyone! Look! It's a man in a dress!" I looked all around me, but I couldn't find whom they were talking about—there were no men in dresses to be found. Besides, even if there had been, how is that remarkable, let alone an insult? It is an article of clothing! It's like saying, "Hey, everyone, look! It's . . . a lamppost!"

Nothing out of the ordinary here, just keep on moving.

I realized that they were, in fact, addressing me when they took out their camera phones to take some shots of me. My heart started to beat faster. My chest tightened. I turned up the music in my headphones. I walked faster.

I did not look back.

This is a disconnect I have come to know well: between what people see and *who I actually am*. I have learned that the most lethal part of the human body is not the fist; it is the eye. What people see and how people see it has everything to do with power.

When I finally reached the grocery store, I still couldn't relax.

The thing about being visibly gender non-conforming is that we are rarely, if ever, defended by other people in public. Everyone thinks that since we "made a choice" to "look like that," we are bringing it upon ourselves. The only reason people can fathom why we would look this way is because we *want to draw attention to ourselves.* They can't even consider that maybe we look like this for ourselves, and not for other people. We are reduced to a spectacle. And when you are a spectacle, the harassment you experience becomes part of the show.

As I checked out my groceries, the person next to me in line approached.

Oh dear, here we go again.

"Hey, can I ask you something?"

I started to walk away.

"Why do you dress like that?"

I stopped in my tracks. This felt like it could be genuine curiosity and not something more hostile.

As I prepared to exit the store, they came a little bit

closer. My heart beat a little bit faster. They lowered their voice.

"It's just that . . . I used to wear skirts and dresses when I was younger."

"What happened?" I asked.

They laughed, but their eyes told another story. There are some questions that have no answers. How do you express pain when you can't even locate the wound?

It's like when you let a balloon loose into the sky. You don't know where it goes, but you know it went somewhere.

Far away.

Over the past few years, we've seen a public dialogue about gender fluidity take place. Most of this conversation has little to do with the everyday experiences of nonbinary people (people who are neither exclusively men nor women) and gender non-conforming people (people who visibly defy society's understanding of what a man or a woman should look like). A lot more airtime is given to other peoples' views of us rather than our own experiences. Our existence is made into a matter of opinion, as if our genders are debatable and not just who we are.

In other words, there's been a lot of talk about us but very little engagement with us. This has led to misinformation and outright lies, which have distracted from the realities faced by gender non-conforming people.

The truth is that we are in a state of emergency. In the past few years, we have seen an onslaught of legislation introduced at the local, state, and federal levels targeting gender non-conforming people by attempting to prohibit curriculum about us, banning us from public accommodations, denying us access to legal protections at work, and barring our access to healthcare. On all fronts—from South Dakota attempting to ban transgender athletes in high school sports; to Tennessee trying to bar us from accessing public spaces, including highways, schools, and parks; to Texas proposing financial compensation for reporting us using the restroom; to legislation across the country permitting businesses the right to deny services on the basis of gender—our communities are under attack. Regardless of whether these pieces of legislation pass, the fact that they are even being considered suggests just how disposable we are considered to be.

These sentiments are also echoed on a federal level. Take, for instance, when the Department of Justice announced that trans and gender non-conforming workers are not protected by civil rights law. Or when the Centers for Disease Control and Prevention censored the word *transgender*. Or, in 2018, when the Department of Health and Human Services attempted to define gender as fixed and binary in a memo that was later leaked. Or the overwhelming opposition to the Equality Act just a year later. The list goes on and on.

Bias and discrimination are not just being endorsed, they are given the green light. This gives many people permission to harass us in public everywhere we go.

The situation is even worse for transfeminine people of color. Despite the ongoing murders of Black transfeminine people, and extreme rates of employment discrimination and homelessness, there has been little societal outcry and action.

At a fundamental level, we are still having to argue for the very ability to exist.

The truth is, I still cannot go outside without being afraid for my safety. There are few spaces where I do not experience harassment for the way I look. Something as simple as running errands leads to strangers interrogating me about my body, trying to find some way to explain why I look like this. "Are you dressed up for a theater production?" "Oh, it must be Fashion Week again!"

I do not have the luxury of being. I am only seen as doing. As if my gender is something that is being done to them and not something that belongs to me. One time I had a waiter come up to me and ask if this was my "Halloween costume" when I was sitting at the table wearing a skirt. It's a surreal experience to have your personhood be reduced to a prop.

How are you supposed to be believed about the harm that you experience when people don't even believe that you exist?

The assumption is that being a masculine man or a feminine woman is normal and that being us is an accessory. Like if you remove our clothing, our makeup, and our pronouns, underneath the surface we are just men and women playing dress up.

The scrutiny on our bodies distracts us from what's really going on here: control. The emphasis on our appearance distracts us from the real focus: power.

⚡   ⚡   ⚡

I grew up in College Station, Texas. When you would fly into our tiny airport, there used to be a sign that read: WELCOME TO COLLEGE STATION, THIS IS COUNTRY! And in this small town, I was part of an even smaller community. Growing up, all the Indians would come together every weekend for a potluck dinner. There weren't that many of us, so we developed a close network. My friends' parents were my aunties and uncles—they were our extended family. There was something about coming together, gossiping, and eating delicious food (we had to drive two hours away just to find our spices!) that made living in this town, so far away from everything that we knew, more tolerable.

At these parties, I used to take my mom's and sister's clothes and promenade around the living room dancing and singing along to the latest Bollywood hits. The ceiling lights in the living room had those fancy dimmers, so with some finesse, you could simulate stage lighting for dramatic effect. Everyone would huddle together, clap, and cheer me on. I'm not sure I was particularly good at the whole dancing part, but I can confirm that I made up in cuteness what I lacked in choreography.

So when the first-grade talent show came around, I had absolutely no inhibitions about signing up. I took to the stage and spun around with reckless abandon: leaping, twirling, skipping, somersaulting—a whole production!

The entire auditorium laughed at me.

It was the first time I remember feeling shame. "Boys don't do that," said my classmates. I couldn't understand why something that gave me so much joy could be met with so much judgment.

Boys don't do *what* exactly? Dance, feel, *somersault*?

I learned about gender through shame. In so many ways, they became inseparable for me. As I grew older, people told me to *stop being so feminine* and *grow up*. Gender non-conformity is seen as something immature, something we have to grow out of to become adults. Overnight, so many of the things that I loved not only became associated with femininity but with shame. Because I was a "boy," I was no longer allowed to want to be a dancer or a fashion designer. Because I was a "boy," I had to stop. Stop dancing. Stop being myself.

Most of this advice was offered with genuine concern. I suppose some people wanted to protect me from bullying and didn't realize that they were bullying me in the process. Others thought this was just part of growing up. But in so many ways, that's what made me even more depressed: how normal it was. How something so painful could be dealt so casually.

The thing about shame is that it eats at you until it fully consumes you. Then you cannot tell the difference between their shame and your own—between a body and an apology. It's not just that you internalize the shame; rather, it becomes you. You no longer need the people at school telling you not to *dress like that*; you already do it to yourself. You no longer need your family telling you to *be quiet*; you already do it to yourself. You edit yourself, and at some point, it becomes so normal that you can't even tell that you're doing it. And the worst part is that you no longer have anyone else to blame.

Eventually the clothing in my closet started to get darker. I threw out all the pinks and florals for cargo shorts. I even tried (rather unsuccessfully) to go Goth. The trouble with being an immigrant kid is that I had to have my parents' approval on what I wore, and they refused to let me shop at Hot Topic. I opted for black sweaters and black slacks instead. The finished look was closer to orchestra recital than hardcore.

Over time I became more and more insecure about every part of my body. My gestures were too "feminine," my voice was too "feminine," my existence was too "feminine." I couldn't listen to recordings of myself without feeling embarrassed, and I hated looking at photos of me. I spent so much time and energy analyzing everything, trying to become as invisible as possible.

The other kids in my school started calling me a sissy and saying that I acted like a girl. Every aspect of myself was analyzed as either "masculine" or "feminine." There was no in-between and nothing outside of these two options. "Why do you have so many friends who are girls?" "Why do you sit like that?" The idea here was that if you were a boy who displayed even a hint of femininity, then you were gay. And if you were gay, then you were wrong. And if you were wrong, that meant they had license to beat you up in the name of morality.

I wasn't really sure what I was, but I knew that I didn't want to be hated. I tried my best to fit in and not draw attention to myself. I tried my best to deepen my voice to talk like the boys, to walk like the boys, and to dress like the boys. But I never felt like I was one of them. Boys' spaces traumatized me because they were where I experienced the most harassment. I didn't go to the restroom in middle school and high school because I was so afraid. As soon as I got home, I would rush to the toilet. This is what happens when fear becomes stronger than need: The body becomes its own closet.

Truth be told, I don't remember much of my childhood because I spent so much of it separated from my body. My body was where the shame lived, so I retreated into my mind. I was bullied everywhere, and it never stopped. It seemed so all consuming, like there was no escape. I became so terrified that my body would betray me—the hint of lavender in my voice, the sparkle in my gesture—so I sought comfort in my head, studying as hard as possible so I could one day get out of my town. I figured that if I was going to be effeminate, then I should at least be smart, to have something redeemable about me.

Looking back, the worst part is I couldn't even talk about what was happening. To speak about the violence would mean acknowledging that I was different from the people around me, which would result in more violence. I couldn't talk to my parents about it because I felt like they would stop loving me if they knew that I was different.

That's the thing about being an LGBTQIA+ kid—you often don't have the luxury to come into yourself on your own terms because other people have made up their minds for you. I wish that my family had been more proactive. I wish they had introduced a conversation about bullying so that I knew I could speak about it happening, too. I wish that they could have let me know that this was not okay.

It took me fifteen more years to embrace my femininity and regain the strength to wear the clothes that I wanted to and not that society told me to. When I started wearing what I wanted to again, it didn't feel like something new, it felt like reclaiming something that I had lost.

It felt like coming home.

After graduating high school, I actively sought out people who questioned everything. I surrounded myself with people who were figuring out who they were, people committed to being vulnerable with one another. I made a home out of long conversations with friends who became my chosen family—people who asked big questions and gave even bigger love.

Eventually I sat down with a couple of my friends and told them that I knew in my heart of hearts that I was not a man nor a woman and that I was physically uncomfortable with the way that I was presenting in the world. I needed to express my femininity more to feel more secure and happy in my body. I said that I was scared that I would have to compromise my safety for my authenticity, but I needed to do this to survive. I couldn't bear being called a man anymore. It hurt too much. Not just in the physical sense but also the spiritual. Life didn't feel worth living. I felt like I had to choose between the impossible options of self-hatred and harassment.

My friends told me that even though I could lose a lot, I never had to worry about losing them.

Surrounded by the people who loved me for me, I realized I finally had other people to support me in my journey. That made all the difference. Even though the bullying never stopped, I finally had people around me to process it with. There's magic in being seen by people who understand—it gives you permission to keep going. Self-expression sometimes requires other people. Becoming ourselves is a collective journey.

I remember the first day I wore a dress in public. I was twenty years old, but I had never felt more giddy and carefree when I walked out of my front door. I stopped thinking about my body and focused on the things around me. It felt like a reunification of my mind, my body, and my spirit—for the first time in a long time, I was able to be completely present with myself and the world. I had so much more energy and motivation. There was a quiet there, a sense of peace in my body, which had for so long been full of anxiety.

I make art—performance poetry, mostly—for a living. As an artist, it is my job to work with the unknown. It is my paint, my canvas, my page, and my stage. What I have learned is that creativity lives in the unfamiliar spaces in our minds. We do not make art from following the rules. We make art precisely from imagining beyond them.

Society's inability to place us in boxes makes them uncomfortable; the unfamiliar becomes a threat and not an opportunity. The unknown calls into question everything that we thought we knew about ourselves and the world.

And this . . . this is a good thing! Being self-reflective and open to transformation is something we should celebrate, not fear.

They used to call me a girl when I was growing up, and when I finally came to accept myself, they called me a boy. I was too feminine to be a boy and then too masculine to be a girl. It's almost as if they move their definitions precisely to exclude us. We are both too much and never enough. We are always made out to be the problem. But maybe we aren't the problem;

maybe the whole gender system is. Whose definitions are we prioritizing, anyway?

The gender binary is set up for us to fail. For us all to fail.

The gender binary is more concerned with gender norms than it is with us. We are led to believe that there are only two genders, "man" and "woman," and these genders are narrow, separate, and opposite. We are taught from a very young age that this is how things have always been and this is the only way to live. We are taught that masculinity belongs to men, femininity belongs to women, and that these are the only two options for self-expression.

Not true.

At its heart, discrimination against gender non-conforming people happens because of a system that rewards conformity and not creativity. Rather than celebrating people who express themselves on their own terms, we repress them. This repression is something we first did to ourselves. We know how to do it so well to other people because we were the first testing grounds. We silenced our own differences, subdued our creativity, and toned down our own gender non-conformity in order to fit in. We thought fitting in would give us security—but is it security when someone else living their life differently unsettles us to our very core?

Repression breeds insecurity breeds violence. When I was in high school, I was tormented for being effeminate. Years after graduating, one of my most vicious bullies sent me a message apologizing for his behavior, revealing that he had since come out as bisexual. Back in school he was jealous and resentful of my freedom of expression and bullied me so that he could prove to other people that he was "normal." It had taken him years to come to terms with his sexuality, and he wanted to apologize for not supporting me with my gender expression back then.

People judge gender non-conformity because they are insecure about their identities. If they weren't, then gender variance wouldn't be so heavily policed. Gender non-conformity causes such a huge reaction because we're consistently taught that there are only two fixed and universal genders. Seeing other people defy this mandate brings the entire system into question.

But there are no such things as gender non-conforming issues; there are just the issues that other people have with themselves, or rather, the issues that they *have with themselves that they take out on us.*

Allow me to explain.

The gender binary is like a party guest who shows up before you get the chance to set the table. Before a baby is even born, well-meaning well-wishers will often ask, "Is it a boy or a girl?" The baby only becomes real to most people once they know the gender. But there are so many more important questions to be asked when a child is born, such as: "How's your baby doing?" or "How can I support you during this time?" or "Why is it so expensive to raise kids?" Or maybe even "Where can I donate to help?"

Babies are born and divided into one of two categories. These categories, boy or girl, affect how we treat the baby when they cry, what clothes we dress the baby in, what toys we allow the baby to play with, and so on. We teach that boys are strong and girls are weak, that boys are aggressive and girls are nice, that boys are rational and girls are emotional. Nothing is spared; we mark everything—the colors, the emotions, the relationships, even the food. And this is done so consistently and with so much authority that we don't even recognize that we are doing it.

At first, these messages might seem trivial, but compounded over time, they become serious. Depending on whether we call them a boy or a girl, we assign each a narrative—we tell some children that they are strong, and we tell others that they are weak. We tell some children that they can express themselves, and we tell others that they should not have feelings. We tell some children that their worth comes from doing harm, and we tell others that their worth comes from accepting it.

And we tell the kids who don't fit into our categories that they are wrong. We tell them that they are not real. We punish them until they conform. We prove that we are real by telling them that they are not. We define ourselves by what we are not.

This gender policing continues when we are adults.

We worry that liking a certain band, hobby, or sport will make us *too* masculine or *too* feminine. We wear pantsuits even when it's blisteringly hot outside, even though skirts would be far more practical. We mock anyone who defies these gender categories.

This is how we prove that we are the genders we say we are: men and women; women and men.

We do the same thing to the next generation that was done to us. We divide billions of people into one of two categories and tell them that this is the way things are. We emphasize and exaggerate the differences between these categories and minimize the differences that exist within them. We forget that there is more variety within the categories of women and men than between them. We forget the ways in which we once deviated from the norm. We forget that humans have never perfectly aligned with these norms.

And yet.

This happens every day, every minute, every second, and we pretend that this is *just the way things are*. And sometimes even that *this is the way things should be*.

People have been so conditioned into believing the status quo that any slight attempt to break free from it brings panic and rage. They think that we are selfish when actually we are imagining a more kind and just world for everyone.

I didn't always think this way.

I recently found some old diaries I wrote when I was figuring out my identity in high school. I wrote about how even though I was attracted to men, I wasn't like *gay people*. I was like *normal* people, I just *happened to be attracted to men*. I wasn't "effeminate" and "womanly," I wasn't "flamboyant" or "obnoxious," I was just a regular person.

Why couldn't I just say who I was without the caveat? Why did there have to be that tension? I needed to put other people down in order to bring myself up. To make myself real, I had to invalidate other people; to make myself right, I had to say other people were wrong. This was my internalized self-hatred on display. At a basic level, I thought that being attracted to men was wrong because it was "feminine," so I had to prove that I was *somehow right*. Conforming to the gender binary was about wanting to hold on to power.

At the time, I thought conforming would make me happier, but instead it just made me more lonely. This is how bullying works: We are afraid of being bullied, so we bully other people. We mistake hurting other people with healing ourselves. We repress ourselves and in turn repress one another, hurting everyone involved.

So often we mistake likability with acceptance. Just because something is more relatable doesn't mean it's better. When the basis of your connection is putting down other people, that connection is going to be weak. There's always the constant fear that people will turn on you. You can never show your vulnerability, because you always have to pretend that you are strong. That's a lot of pressure.

True acceptance doesn't look like having to change who you are in order to be embraced. Conditional acceptance is not freedom—we shouldn't have to erase our differences in order to be respected.

It took years of self-work, of meeting other gender non-conforming people, of reading and learning my own history to recognize that I was saying these things from a place of deep self-hatred and shame. This is how shame works: It recruits you into doing its work for you. It's a chain reaction. Our parents shamed us because their parents shamed them because theirs shamed them, and so on. A cycle of violence.

Reclaiming my body, my identity, and my worth back from other people's shame has showed me that transformation is possible, no matter how impossible it may seem.

I receive *a lot* of hate on social media. As a visibly gender non-conforming person of color, a lot of people go out of their way to insult me. Sometimes they send me throw-up emojis and GIFs of people vomiting. The idea here is that my appearance is so disgusting that it makes people sick at the very sight of me. But on the other hand, I also receive so much support. Every week people message me saying that at first, they were uncomfortable with my photos, but after a while they took the time to reconsider their biases and now totally don't care about what I look like. Oftentimes they say that the reason they had such a strong reaction to my image was because of their own bodily insecurity—and by learning to accept my gender non-conformity, they became more comfortable with themselves.

The thing about disgust is that it makes prejudice physical. And just because something is physical doesn't mean that it's *natural*. In fact, our bodies are trained to respond to certain things over others. Learned behaviors can also be *unlearned*: it's possible to develop more kind and just ways of relating to ourselves and one another. What we look like isn't gross; what is truly disgusting is how we shame one another for our physical appearances.

We do remarkable things with jealousy and fear. Rather than naming them and acknowledging when we are operating from them, we repress them and pretend they aren't there. Jealousy, even when disguised with big language, is still jealousy—an emotion that makes both you and me small. Others will project their insecurity on you because it is easier than dealing with their internal pain.

⚡   ⚡   ⚡

Power can be defined as the ability to make a particular perspective seem universal. Control is how power maintains itself; anyone who expresses another perspective is punished. Arguments against gender non-conforming people are about maintaining power and control. Most can be grouped into four categories: dismissal, inconvenience, biology, and the slippery slope. These are strategies that people use to make the gender binary seem like a given, not a decision. It's important to understand how they work in order to imagine otherwise.

Dismissal

In order to even get a seat at the table, people have to believe that you exist. When it comes to gender non-conforming people, we are still at square one—still having to argue that we are real. What's never questioned here is, whose standards of authenticity are we being held up to in the first place?

"It's common sense that everyone is a man or a woman."

Common sense is what happens when a particular point of view is regarded as the status quo because it's held by the people in power, not necessarily because it is right. These perspectives are told so often that we begin to see them as universal truths. We accept the fact that this is the way things are and have always been. For large periods of history, it was "common sense" that Black people and people of color were inferior and that this supposed inferiority justified discrimination, genocide, and slavery. Just because an opinion is widely held does not make it right.

"Why use the pronoun *they* when it's plural? It's not grammatically correct."

Despite the fact that in 2019 Merriam-Webster added the gender-neutral *they* pronoun to the dictionary, people are still upset about the use of a singular *they*.

People's fixation on "proper" grammar or "new terms" often hides a more sinister motive, even if it's not conscious. They are okay with language shifting as long as it's the people in power doing it, not us. They say that gender non-conforming people, in particular, are caught up on some new fad: that we are inventing language, identities, pronouns, and genders. But language and grammar have always been developed to meet the needs of society. Consider words like *selfie* and *welp*, which have recently been added to the dictionary. This is actually the purpose of language— to give meaning to concepts as they evolve.

They is not exclusively plural and actually does have a history of being used as a singular pronoun in the English language. In fact, many people still use it unconsciously today. For example, when you find a lost phone and have no idea who it belongs to, you might say, "Did somebody leave their phone behind?"

The selective outcry over new words to describe gender and sexuality—amidst the thousands of words that are added to the dictionary every year—is about prejudice, not principle. If these people are so averse to change, why aren't they outlawing the use of *bingeable* or taking more public stances on the use of the Oxford comma?

"This gender nonbinary and gender-fluid thing is just a new youth Internet fad. There are only two genders."

While the actual words might be new, living beyond the gender binary is not. Indigenous people and people outside the Western world have long existed outside of the gender binary: two-spirit among American Indians, hijra in South Asia, waria in Indonesia, muxe in Mexico, just to name a few. In many of these societies, people living outside of the binary were and continue to be recognized as leaders. It's not that these people do not exist, it's that they have been erased to make the Western gender binary seem like the only option, and not a particular and specific cultural worldview. What is regarded as masculine and feminine is not set in stone but actually shifts across time, culture, and space. Even in the Western world, pink was once considered a masculine color and heels were actually first worn by men!

"You are not normal. You have a disorder that needs to be fixed."

It's important to understand the difference between being "normal" and being "normative." Being normal means that a numerically significant amount of something is found in a group. For example, if you select a random group of students, chances are a large percentage will be wearing sneakers. This is normal. Being *normative* is about what gets elevated by society to a position of power. Normativity looks like a specific sneaker brand being upheld as the best. Normativity, then, is about value judgment and shouldn't be used interchangeably with *normal*.

It's not that gender non-conforming people aren't

normal, it's that we aren't considered normative. Gender diversity is a natural attribute of human expression, not an illness that needs to be fixed. Gender non-conforming people face considerable distress not because we have a disorder, but because of stigma and discrimination. There is nothing wrong with us, what is wrong is a world that punishes us for not being normatively masculine or feminine. Increasing acknowledgment of this reality is why groups like the World Health Organization, the World Medical Association, and the American Psychological Association have formally depathologized gender-diverse identities.

"You want to be different to draw attention to yourselves. Hurt feelings aren't real discrimination."

This outright ignores the disproportionately high rates of murder, physical violence, job discrimination, homelessness, and health gaps among gender non-conforming people. According to the 2015 US Transgender Survey, 30 percent of trans and gender non-conforming people reported workplace discrimination resulting in an unemployment rate of three times more than the general population; 23 percent of respondents experienced housing discrimination; and 77 percent of respondents experienced mistreatment in school. Gender non-conforming people are not opportunisitic; we are *oppressed*.

Pain does not have to be visible to be real, and violence does not have to be physical to be serious. Imagine everyone you encounter all day long telling you that you are not real and that there is something fundamentally wrong with you. Being constantly invalidated takes a toll: 40 percent of trans and gender non-conforming people have attempted suicide. Emotional and physical violence are not in competition with each other. It is possible to acknowledge one without invalidating the other.

Inconvenience

Okay. So people might tolerate the existence of gender non-conforming people, but tolerance is not the same thing as acceptance. Tolerance is always about maintaining distance: "This is about something over there that doesn't concern me." Acceptance, on the other hand, is about integrating difference into your own life: "This is about something that I'm a part of, and I need to learn more to better help." True acceptance can be uncomfortable at first, precisely because it takes work. Unfortunately, many people would rather prioritize their own comfort over our livelihood.

"You are an insignificant minority."

As of 2016, there are 1.4 million openly transgender people in the United States, and that's hardly insignificant. Also, it's important to remember that most people cannot express their gender without legitimate fear of rejection, losing their homes and jobs (if they even have them), and significant violence. Since most people cannot express their gender publicly because of safety concerns, we do not actually know how many trans and gender non-conforming people there are.

**"You are making everything about gender.
Stop bringing it up if you want it to go away."**

This is ironic because we are actually trying to
make gender *less* relevant. It's curious where society
locates the blame. What about the gender-reveal
parties, the birth certificates, the gendered sections
at clothing stores, the driver's licenses, all the ways
that society imposes gender on us all? When things
like this are normalized, they become invisible and
we don't even question them. Critiquing gender is not
the same thing as creating gender. Not talking about
it won't make gender inequality go away; in fact, that's
precisely how this injustice persists.

**"Why be nonbinary? Why can't you just be
feminine men or masculine women?
Things are just getting unnecessarily
complicated with all these options."**

Some gender non-conforming people are
nonbinary, and some are men and women. It depends
on each person's experience. Two people can look
similar and be completely different genders. Gender

is not what people look like to other people; it is what we know ourselves to be. No one else should be able to tell you who you are; that's for you to decide. Rather than considering the existence of multiple genders as a bad thing or even a good thing, why do we need moral judgment of it altogether? There are many ways that people can exist and describe themselves. Why is that a problem? We don't consider remembering everyone's individual name a burden; we just accept that as the way things work. Gender should be the same way.

"I get that you're different, but why do you need to shove it in my face? Keep it to yourselves."

People think their discomfort is just like the discrimination we face. This is a false equivalency. Often this distress arises because people are having their authority challenged. Consider this: We live in a society that presumes everyone as heterosexual and binary gendered before giving them a chance to come into themselves. Society asks—no, demands—that

LGBTQIA+ people agree with this and be exposed to it through our curriculums and television screens. When we ask for even a fraction of this consideration, we are seen as too much. This is a prejudiced double standard.

"Gender neutrality erases my right to be a woman or a man."

Calling for recognition of nonbinary people is not the same thing as requiring everyone to be nonbinary. Drawing attention to issues facing nonbinary people does not erase the struggles women face. This is not a zero-sum game and there is enough room for everyone. Gender-neutral language isn't about replacing an old norm with a new one. People have the right to self-determine their gender whether it be a man, woman, or a nonbinary gender. The goal of gender-neutral language is to get rid of gender normativity, not everyone's gender. While gendered language might be helpful to describe individual experiences, gender-neutral language helps us be more inclusive when talking about groups. Individual men and women have valid experiences as men and women, but these cannot necessarily be generalized. For example, when we say that women give birth, we neglect that some women are not capable of giving birth while some trans men and nonbinary people are. The gender-neutral alternative "people who give birth" holds all of these realities just like the gender-neutral "siblings" includes brothers, sisters, and nonbinary siblings. Using gender-neutral language isn't about being politically correct, it's just about being correct.

Biology

The word *biological* actually has nothing to do with gender or even an original state of being. It just means pertaining to living matter. But some people use the word *biological* to position trans and gender non-conforming people as artificial and everyone else as natural. This is part of a larger system of using science as a rhetorical strategy for a normative goal. There is absolutely no biological basis for why boys should not paint their nails or be sensitive and girls should not play football or be taken seriously for their ideas. This is not about science, it's about power.

"You can't dispute the reality of science!"

Science and biology are still products of human culture and do not exist outside of it. It used to be common medical practice in the United States to measure skull size to determine intelligence, along with a whole host of procedures that have since been debunked. Societal beliefs about sex affect what questions scientists ask and the knowledge they gain. Scientific knowledge is not fixed—it shifts as cultural prejudice is revealed and challenged. Oftentimes we associate "scientific knowledge" with knowledge itself, dismissing everything else as just opinion. This science-opinion binary is oversimplified, especially when it comes to issues of gender and sexuality. One of the ways in which our society produces the gender binary is by exaggerating findings based on shaky evidence that has been widely condemned by professionals. In 2018, in response to pervasive anti-trans legislation, over 2,500 distinguished scientists released a statement noting that the idea of the gender binary has no biological basis. Everyday people without adequate training pretend to be scientific experts. This doesn't reveal much about gender, but it does demonstrate the lengths that people go to in order to distort reality to serve their purposes.

"I agree that gender is cultural but sex is biological."

People say that while we might be able to change our gender, our sex is always set because it's based on our biology. The belief that the category of sex is fixed and purely biological reflects an overly simplistic perspective of science and society. Biology and culture are yet another false binary. Nothing exists in a cultural vacuum. Sex is not only biological, it is also cultural. And just because something is cultural doesn't make it less real. For example, money—pieces of paper—does not have inherent value or meaning, but nonetheless still has major consequences on our lives.

Scientific definitions of sex are not a given; they

shift drastically over time. The idea that humans have a binary sex is a relatively recent phenomenon from the 1700s. Before then, it was a widely held belief by experts that humans were inherently both male and female. In the nineteenth century, scientists believed that binary sex was only possible in white people, who were seen as more "advanced" than other races. Today, conversations about binary sex erase intersex people who are born outside the binaries of male or female altogether. The fact that doctors still perform non-consensual and non-medically necessary surgeries on intersex people just because they are different shows how binary sex—like binary gender—is a political construction. These people are not accidents or malfunctions; this is how human diversity works.

Ideas of gender, sex, race, and citizenship are constantly being redefined. When it comes to gender and sex, definitions are constantly drawn as a means to exclude us. They used to define *sex* as what was reflected on an individual's birth certificate. Once that was changeable, they made the definition our genitalia. Once we could change those, the definition switched to chromosomes. Now that there is increasing evidence that chromosomes do not always necessarily align with sex, they are suggesting genetic testing. This is not about science—this is about targeted prejudice.

"We all have an innate tendency for the gender binary because this is how humans reproduce."

First off, this claim has long been used as a tool of discrimination. People in power make hierarchies and stereotypes seem natural in order to make inequality seem inevitable and permanent. For a long time, and even sometimes today, women were incorrectly seen as innately prone to the condition of hysteria, an association which has long barred women from accessing certain professions. This "biological basis" was used to justify why only men were allowed in certain work fields.

Second, people of all genders can and do reproduce. Having a father and a mother is only one way to define family. Not the only way. Often critics of gender non-conforming people are more concerned with the conception of life than they are with the care and social structures needed to sustain it. It takes a lot of coordinated work to maintain life: providing shelter, guidance, protection, food, and care. There are many ways to support life beyond and outside of sexual reproduction—roles that LGBTQIA+ people have long been a part of across cultures.

"There are undeniable differences between male bodies and female bodies."

While it is true that there are bodily differences, it is a political choice to emphasize certain differences over others in order to create categories. For example, humans have more in common with monkeys than monkeys do with . . . octopuses, yet we call them both animals and us humans. Body hair and body shape vary within genders. There are many women with body hair and facial hair and many men without it. Not all women are able to bear children and not all men are physically strong. There are many men with curves and many women without them. Differences and the variation within categories are glossed over to exaggerate differences between sexes.

"You must have gender dysphoria and pursue medical transition to be legitimately trans."

Some transgender people experience incredible distress from the disconnect between their external bodies and their internal senses of self, and some transgender people do not. Some transgender people are men or women, and some are nonbinary. It is possible to hold both these truths without disqualifying or discrediting one or the other. In fact, standardizing only *one way* to be transgender is reductive. While we are beginning to recognize a plurality of ways to be a man or a woman, we still have such limited understandings of what it means to be transgender. This is because transgender narratives are often determined by the medical establishment, rather than our own experiences. There are trans women and trans men who do not medically transition and are no less authentic. There are nonbinary people who do pursue hormones and surgery, and they are not more authentic. Medical intervention does not make trans people more "real" than others, and it should be a personal choice, not a societal mandate. This type of thinking is especially dangerous when gender-inclusive healthcare is so expensive and inaccessible to most trans and nonbinary people across the world.

Trans people are diverse and complex. Our experiences of our genders and bodies do not need to be universal to be valid. Being real is not a scarce resource, and it is possible to hold a diversity of experiences without creating hierarchies.

Slippery Slope

People use slippery slope arguments when they believe that an idea or a course of action will lead to something wrong or disastrous. Often situations that are completely unrelated become associated with one another. The problem with this line of thinking is that fear and panic cause people to take illogical jumps and make connections between topics that don't actually line up. Rather than focusing on the topic at hand, they bring up something totally different.

"If we allow people to self-determine their genders, then pretty soon people are going to start identifying as frying pans or anything, you name it."

This is an age-old strategy that was used against the women's movement and the civil rights movement that dodges addressing the issue by derailing the conversation. What we are arguing for is people's self-determination of gender—an approach that has long been practiced in societies across time and place.

"If we allow people to self-determine their genders, then anyone can say that they are a man or a woman!"

What's behind this fear is an assumption that there is one stable and shared experience of manhood or womanhood and that if we move beyond this one definition, *man* and *woman* will stop having meaning. But the fact of the matter is that there are many experiences of manhood and womanhood. No individual woman experiences all the issues that every woman can go through. A wealthy white woman has a fundamentally different experience of womanhood than a working-class woman of color. A man born in Paris, France, has a different experience than one born in Paris, Texas. There is as much (if not more) difference within the category of woman than there is between men and women. *Man* and *woman* don't lose their meaning when we recognize the diversity and difference within them; rather, they invite us to be more specific.

"If we provide protections and accommodations on the basis of gender identity, then women will be harmed."

The 2015 US Transgender Survey found that about one in ten trans and gender non-conforming people were physically attacked in the past year, and nearly half are survivors of sexual violence. The numbers are likely higher because of underreporting. Trans and gender non-conforming people are actually more likely to be assaulted while using public accommodations, not the other way around.

This is a deliberate strategy of using feminist

rhetoric as a smokescreen to cover up anti-trans bigotry. Trans and gender non-conforming rights *are* women's rights because many trans and gender non-conforming people are also women. The irony is, then, that people are misusing the language of women's rights *specifically to harm women.*

"If we can't define gender, then how will we be able to legislate around it?"

Just because something is difficult doesn't mean it's impossible. Laws, like language and culture, have to shift and adapt over time to address the needs of society, and it's time to create new policies and protocols that move beyond the gender binary. This is about who we prioritize and who we see as disposable. If gender non-conforming people were taken seriously and not dismissed as a conspiracy, people would spend less time panicking about the future of the legal system and more time being concerned with the injustices we face today.

What you begin to notice in having these conversations is that they accuse us of doing the very things that they are doing to us.

They say that we are erasing them

> as they actively erase the long history of cultures outside the Western gender binary.

They say that we are making things up

> as they invent hundreds of new laws to legislate us out of existence.

They say that we are pretending

> as they recite the scripts about gender they have been taught.

They say that we are attacking them

> as hate crimes against trans and gender non-conforming people increase.

This is how power works: It makes the actual people experiencing violence seem like a threat. Moving from a place of fear leads us to make harmful assumptions about one another. In our fear, we treat other people's identities as if they are something that they are doing to us *and not something that just exists.*

The world we want is one in which all people, regardless of their appearances, are treated with dignity and respect—one in which these factors do not have a bearing on safety, employment, and opportunity. We want a world that acknowledges and appreciates the complexity of everyone and everything—one in which transformation is celebrated and not repressed. We want a world where people have an underlying worth regardless of their gender.

The gender binary is hurting us all, and it is time for us to finally put it to rest. Harm from the gender binary looks different for all of us: It can look like the person at the grocery store who no longer feels comfortable wearing dresses, it can look like a woman being called aggressive for speaking her mind or ugly for not shaving her legs, it can look like a man being called weak for not wanting to fight or not being believed for experiencing harm, and it can look like me getting spat on simply for being in public. It can look like all of us not feeling worthy, real, and beautiful because we are constantly comparing ourselves to the norms we have been taught.

We want a world where boys can feel, girls can lead, and the rest of us can not only exist but thrive. This is not about erasing men and women but rather acknowledging that man and woman are two of many—stars in a constellation that do not compete but amplify one another's shine.

Gender is a story, not just a word. There are as many ways to be a woman as there are women. There are as many ways to be a man as there are men. There are as many ways to be nonbinary as there are nonbinary people. This complexity is not chaos, it just is. We do not need to be universal to be valid. We should be able to decide what the clothes and the colors we adorn, the bodies we inhabit, and the people we love mean to *us*. There should be no boys' clothes or girls' clothes, just clothes. Separating gender from norms creates infinite possibilities for us all—we get to narrate what our bodies, experiences, and interests mean. Without the gender binary, there will be no more restrictive definitions of woman and man, and masculinity and femininity. Instead, there will just be *your* definition—one of many. Objects, emotions, and careers will not be "masculine" or "feminine," but they will be "adventurous" or "compassionate." We will develop more precise language to describe ourselves and the beauty around us, more just practices to respect ourselves and one another.

Imagine how beautiful it would be if the way we navigated the world was about creative expression, not conforming to arbitrary norms.

I often think about how much time and work it takes to sustain the gender binary. How much we have to repress—all the feelings and dreams we have to sacrifice on account of *proving* that we are real. To prove that we are real, we have to dismiss everything different about ourselves and develop so many big words and justifications to disguise our insecurity. We sacrifice what they call feminine so that we can be masculine, and we sacrifice what they call masculine so that we become feminine. We spend so much time trying to make other people comfortable that oftentimes we don't even know what makes us happy. It's exhausting.

Our movement is restricted (don't walk like that, you look _____), our voices stifled (don't speak like that, you sound _____), our creativity repressed (don't dress like that, you look _____), our romance dismissed (don't love like that, you feel _____), our behavior belittled (don't act like that, you seem _____).

Sometimes when I am facilitating creative-writing workshops, I give a prompt to my participants: "What part of yourself did you have to destroy in order to survive in this world?"

I was terrified that when I came into myself, I would lose everything. Instead, I found myself. I found the connection I had been searching for my entire life: people who loved me for me and not my category; beauty in my individuality, not my obedience.

Over time, I learned that where I was taught

dissonance, I found harmony. This beard, this skirt, this love: There are no contradictions here, there is just someone trying to figure it out. Someone very similar to and very different from you.

Tomorrow you could wake up and feel inspired to wear your first lipstick or suit (or both!). Next year you could fall in love with someone you never thought you would. Ten years from now you could have a major realization and decide to transition genders. Who knows what the future holds? We should not hold ourselves back for the sake of convention. Instead, we should embrace ongoing transformation as a necessary part of what it means to be alive.

ABOUT US

Pocket Change Collective was born out of a need for space. Space to think. Space to connect. Space to be yourself. And this is your invitation to join us.

These books are small, but they are mighty. They ask big questions and propose even bigger solutions. They show us that no matter where we come from or where we're going, we can all take part in changing the communities around us. Because the possibilities of how we can use our space for good are endless.

So thank you. Thank you for picking this book up. Thank you for reading. Thank you for being a part of the Pocket Change Collective.